My Crazy Grandpa And The Book That Saved His Life

Written By Queon Blackman

Illustrated By Tya White

Dedication

Firstly, all praises are due to Allah.

To my wife, the love of my life, the crown mother, you have been the perfect partner that has supported me and made me better as a man. To my mother and father for pouring the love that you poured into me. And my children, daddy loves you. Also, shoutout to my life long friend Hamzah, who gave me my first real introduction to the faith.

As'salamu Alaikum.

On our way to my grandpa's house I complained. I complained ALL the way. It's not that I don't like grandpa, but it's hard to believe he likes me.

"He barely speaks mom. All he does is grunts and makes old man noises when he climbs out of his chair. I don't think he likes kids."

"He likes kids Tajmah." my mom said through her laughter, "He just has a different way of expressing his love. He's an old man that has a lot of life experience. Your grandpa is very interesting. You should ask him how a book saved his life."

"What do you mean?" I asked.

"Ask him yourself. The book is on top of a tall bookshelf."

As my father parked the car you can sense the excitement in both he and my mother. You must have to be an adult to appreciate the subtle, snarky remarks or comments from grandpa. Nonetheless I mentally prepared myself for what was to come. We approached the door with my baggage. After the door opened, my parents lit up. There were smiles, hugs, and laughter. Then grandpa looked at me and asked, "Who is this little human?"

A rush of warmth ran through my face. Do I say my name? Do I laugh? My mom whispered to me, "Say hi."

I said, "Hi." Then he hugged me. He smelled like vapor rub and fresh depends.

The house smelled like food. As soon as it hit my nose, I was ready to eat. He made chili. Mom told me that he was somewhat of a cook, so expectations were *somewhat* high. Grandpa guided us to the room I would be staying in for the night. The smell of the food was seriously haunting my nose the entire time. We dropped off my things and to the kitchen we went. Mom, dad, and I sat at the kitchen table as he prepared our food. My father asked, "How is your day so far, pop?" In which grandpa responded, "I had a nice bowel movement earlier." They all laughed as my mom implored him not to make inappropriate jokes while preparing our food. He didn't disappoint. The food was delicious.

I excused myself to go to the bathroom. As I walked past a hall, I saw it in my peripheral vision. I stopped and took a step back. There it was, isolated on top of the tall bookshelf. The book that saved this crazy old man's life. I can tell it was old.

Older than me. It looks like it's been through some things. It was dark green. The sides of the pages look golden. I couldn't quite make out the words on the spine, but the most interesting thing about this book is that it had a stab through the cover. That's right, a knife stabbing. It intrigued me. I need to know what happened.

After using the restroom, I returned to the table. Before I
continued eating, I asked, "Grandpa, how did that book save
your life?"

He said, "Well, where do I begin, little human?" His response prompted my dad to say, "We'll let you guys discuss that. We're headed out." My parents were going on a date for the whole day. A day date. I wonder what they're going to do. I can sense the glee in their spirit to be getting rid of me for a day. It's a bit annoying but at the same time, gratifying. I'm glad they found some time to be happy. I guess even adults need to find time for themselves. I hugged my parents goodbye and they were off. They said that they will pick me up tonight. Whatever. Grandpa and I saw them off and headed back to the table. I thought to myself, back to business old man. I've got some questions, and I want answers.

"So, Grandpa, how did that book save your life, and where did the stabbing come from?" I asked.

"Well, Tajmah *that book* is called the Qur'an."

Oh, the Qur'an! My intrigue spiked. I've seen plenty of Qur'ans in my twelve years on this Earth. Not one had been stabbed! I mean, I've heard my parents speak on the subtle difficulties and challenges of being Muslim in America. They also would lecture about the difficulties of being black. Blah, blah, blah. A question as simple as, "What year was the 4th of July?" would have me trapped in a 30 min long discussion on slavery and some dude called Douglas Fredrick, or whatever. Mom seemed to be calm and cool when these topics came up. My father was different. He seemed triggered or something. I wonder which one I will be when I grow up.

I'm sure one day this info would be important to me, but for now I just need to know the answer to this last question on my homework. 1776 is all I need. A stabbed Qur'an is actually kind of dramatic.

He paused and looked past my head into space. Almost as if he was looking into infinity or into the past itself and looking directly into the events as they happened. Grandpa continued.

"I remember the first time I was given *that book*. In the beginning, I was in the 7th grade. We were learning nothing, when a new kid was escorted into class. His name was Adam. I didn't think much of him until I got home. You see, there was a house in my neighborhood that had been vacant for some time. After school, I noticed a family had moved in, and wouldn't you know it, it was Adam's family.

At this point, who would have thought that he was to become a lifelong friend. Our initial interactions were through basketball. He had a basketball hoop in the front of his house and through this game our friendship began and grew. Our conversations naturally expanded beyond basketball. We started discussing family, video games, movies and religion. He said he was a Muslim.

Now, up to this point I vaguely heard of a Muslim. I know they follow something called Islam, worshiped someone called Allah, and follow some book called the Qur'an. I was intrigued. I asked questions. The more I asked, the more I wanted to know. He was happy to answer. He eventually offered me a Qur'an. It was green. The sides of the pages were

golden. It was in good condition."

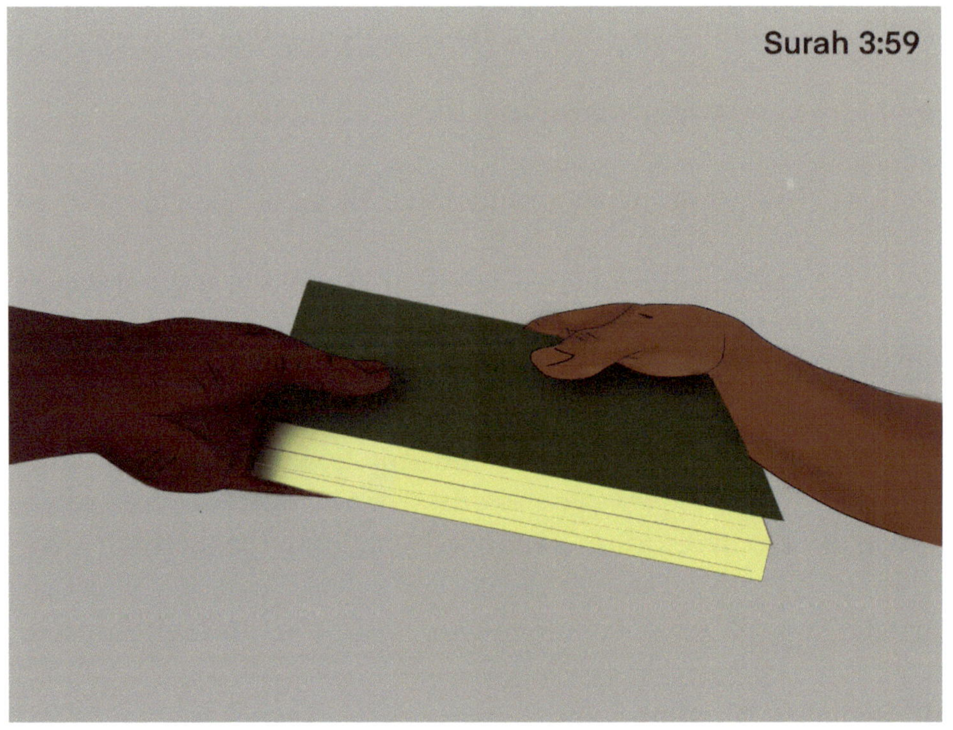

"So, that's where you got it from." I said, "Did you read

it right away or…?"

He said he read it every now and again. Okay, so I know what

the book is and how he got it. I was not expecting it to be the

Qur'an, but he still had not told me how it got stabbed. I have a feeling this is going to be a while. I'm going to have to be patient, but I wish he would spit it out already.

He continued, "I didn't read much at first, because when we were young, we actually played outside. There was none of that insta-face or gram-book. All the kids played outside. I remember these brothers in particular. They used to always bicker and fight. Their names were Corey and Andrew.

Corey and Andrew fought like many other siblings. Sometimes the fights got more extreme than others. One day while we were playing basketball, things got a little too contentious and Corey ended up throwing a rock at Andrew. It hit him directly in the head. That was kind of crazy. He bled and cried. He was taken to the hospital where he gotten stitches. To see someone do that to their own brother was disheartening. All that blood…"

He concluded his story with that word, blood. It gave me little chills. Not the word, but how he said it. Along with his face. In a way, he was able to display vulnerability. This is the first time I've seen it in him. I didn't really see it often in my father either. My father would say, "As a black man, it's okay to display emotion and even cry. But there's a time and a place."

"When do *you* cry daddy?" I asked. In which he simply responded, "A time and a place." At this point I realize how good of a storyteller my grandfather is. But he still hasn't answered the question. He answers questions as slow as he walks or gets out of his chair. He has my attention though.

He arose from the dining room table and offered me something to drink, "Water or juice?". I can tell he just needed a break. An intermission if you will. I opted for juice. He poured himself water, sat down, and continued.

"I remember trying to read the Qur'an here and there. One of the most interesting things about Islam, initially, was the people who had some association with the faith. One of the greatest basketball players to ever play was Kareem Abdul-Jabbar. One of the greatest boxers to ever box was Muhammad Ali. And one of the greatest orators to ever speak, Malcolm X.

All these people fascinated me. Not only were they all great, but they also just so happen to speak to my people in a very grasping way. Not from an angle of weakness or desperation, but from a place of strength. When others seemed to be begging for respect, the Muslims demanded it. It made me feel… empowered.

In the 8th grade my family and I went on a trip. I was told it was a road trip, so I figured I'd bring the book. This is the first time I was able to read a big chunk of it at once. It turns out it wasn't just a road trip. We pulled up to a park where we could go white water rafting."

"Oh, wow grandpa! I've never done that before!" I exclaimed.

"What was it like?" Grandpa looked down, paused for about 2 seconds, and finally looked back up.

He said, "Well Tajmah, I don't know what it's like."

Again, there goes the vulnerability. Hesitantly, I asked "What happened?" I immediately felt a bit afraid of the answer because of the shift in his energy.

Grandpa answered, "Before we went rafting ourselves, we decided to watch others. Now, I don't know whose job it is to watch the flow of the waters. It seemed there should be someone to determine if the river is too dangerous. I say this because the waters picked up.

The river went from calm and placid, to extreme and rapid. This all happened very quickly. All of a sudden, a raft with six people came around the bend. It was dangerous. You can see the people on the raft realize they were in trouble. The waters were out of control. All of a sudden, one of the young men bounced out of the raft! My heart dropped. People around gasped. Some even screamed. There was a young man no more than 17 or 18 years old. He was wearing a life vest but the waters were very violent. He was hit with aggressive waves over and over again, struggling to get air. The waves smacked him in the face. You can feel the suffocation. He slid under the water and drifted ahead of the raft. He came out of the water onto a boulder.

It was a slight relief to see him there, but it was obvious that his life was still in peril. As the raft approached the boulder, you can hear a man on the raft yell 'Son!' The yell was chilling. He reached out a hand for his son, but the young man was just too afraid to release his mighty grip on the rock.

He gave no attempt to leave the rock, and the raft passed him by. That's when everyone including me realized, his opportunity for a long-fulfilled life passed by also. One final wave hit this young man, and we never saw him again."

Tears started rolling down my face. When my mom said that grandpa had a lot of life experience, she wasn't lying. He was only in the 8th grade and had witnessed a dramatic death already. This conversation has taken a turn that I wasn't expecting.

"That's so sad grandpa." I said. He agreed. He then made it a point to let me know that good things happen too. To prove this point he started right into another story.

"One day while we were eating dinner, we heard a fire truck go past our house. Being that we lived in a small neighborhood, it piqued our interest. To our surprise, there was a fire a few houses down. It was an imposing sight to behold. The fire was both astonishing and scary at the same time.

Other neighboring families also congregated to see the fire. More emergency vehicles arrived. The people who lived in the house stood outside looking at their home, in a blaze. The mother of the house was hysterical. She was attempting to go inside. Apparently, there was someone still in the home. They held her from approaching. While they did that, a fireman ran into the flame infested house. The woman yelled, 'My baby!'

I began to feel goosebumps and chills run through my arms. I was thinking something terrible was going to happen again. My mother recognized that something bad could transpire, so she began moving me towards our home. Just as she did, the fireman ran out with a toddler in his arms. He put the child on the ground, and the young boy ran to his mother. To my astonishment this boy was unharmed and seemingly untouched. The crowd cheered."

Oh wow. Finally, a story that ended positively. He decided to take a break on that good note and suggested I go to the store with him. Well, he made it seem like a suggestion, but really it was more of a demand.

On our drive to the store grandpa played music. He sang, he whistled, he even danced a little. His love for music was clear. I noticed sometimes when a song began, he would begin reciting the lyrics before the actual artist did. It was as if he loved it so much he couldn't hold back his excitement to get it out.

Shopping with grandpa was like shopping with dad. Just much slower. Even the way he walked. He, like my father, had a sort of bounce in his walk. Again, much slower. After we got back in the car. I asked him why do black men walk like that? "As the original man, we walk with the rhythm of the earth."

Hmmm. Interesting. Throughout the ride home, I had more questions in between people singing about grapevines and wishing it would rain. He didn't have an answer to every question. "Answers aren't always revealed to us." he said, "Those that say don't know, and those that know don't say."

It was such a fun conversation. Most of his answers were vague and riddle-like. We arrived back to the house to the sound of Sam Cooke singing about a gang of men working in chains. A Chain Gang.

While putting the groceries away grandpa accidentally dropped a can of string beans. Just before he bent down to grab them, I stopped him. "Hey, hey, hey!" I exclaimed. "I'll get it, old man. I don't want you getting stuck down there." He smiled. He appreciated it. Not the help. The humor. I get it now.

As he cooked, he told me many more amazing stories. He told me these astonishing events that he experienced intertwined with his readings of the Qur'an. There were good stories, bad stories, happy and sad. One thing is for certain and two things for sure, this is a very interesting old man. After my mom told me how interesting he is, I didn't imagine I would be so emotionally invested in this old man and so consumed in his stories.

I expressed to him how amazing his life was. He chuckled and said, "Yea, I've been through a lot. Life can be so tough. It can be tough physically, mentally, emotionally, and above all, spiritually. You want to know what helped me through it all? The Qur'an. Its teachings kept my mind and emotions straight and grounded to maneuver through life. If it wasn't for that book, I wouldn't have survived this chaos. The Qur'an saved my life."

He had more to say about the Qur'an. He was especially fascinated by the prophets and their stories. It's amazing how their stories had lessons within them and these lessons helped him in life. He expressed that these stories were very important in his journey to becoming a better person.

And there you have it. It took all day, but I finally understand why this book is so important to my grandpa and how it saved his life. This day had effects on me that I didn't expect. I started to think deeply about myself and my religion. Somehow this crazy old man made me extra proud to be black and Muslim. After deep thought I went to my bag and retrieved my hijab. I went to the mirror and put it on, proudly.

Soon after I fell asleep, I was awakened by my parents late at night. They greeted me with "As'salamu Alaikum." and said "We're going home." Grandpa walked us out to the car.

We hugged and said our goodbyes. Just as the car started to pull off something suddenly came to my mind. I never learned where the stabbing came from! I yelled, "WAIT!" My father stopped the car. I poked my head out of the window and said, "Hey old man, you never told me where that stabbing came from."

"Oh, that? I was walking home from a friend's house. The sun had already fallen. I had on a hoodie with a pouch. A guy came out of the darkness. He had a small knife and stabbed me right in the stomach and ran off. Well, fortunately for me I had the Qur'an in my pouch. So, the Qur'an took the brunt of the blow, and I escaped with just a cut. Allahu Akbar."

END